21st
Century
Skills Library

COOL ARTS CAREERS

CHOREOGRAPHER

KATIE MARSICO

Published in the United States of America by
Cherry Lake Publishing, Ann Arbor, Michigan
www.cherrylakepublishing.com

Content Adviser
Ginger Jensen, Artistic Director and Founder,
Renegade Dance Architects, Chicago, Illinois

Credits
Cover and pages 1 and 24, ©iStockphoto.com/craftvision; pages 4, 10, 17, 18,
22, and 28, ©ASSOCIATED PRESS; page 7, ©iStockphoto.com/oleg66; page 8,
©Jan Sochor/Alamy; pages 9 and 14, ©ilian ballet/Alamy; page 12, ©moodboard/
Alamy; page 13, ©ilian travel/Alamy; page 21, ©Jose Gil/Dreamstime.com;
page 26, ©iStockphoto.com/Gerville

Library of Congress Cataloging-in-Publication Data
Marsico, Katie, 1980–
  Choreographer/by Katie Marsico.
    p. cm.—(Cool arts careers)
  Includes bibliographical references and index.
  ISBN-13: 978-1-61080-136-2 (lib. bdg.)
  ISBN-10: 1-61080-136-9 (lib. bdg.)
  1. Choreography—Juvenile literature. 2. Choreographers—Vocational
guidance—Juvenile literature. I. Title.
  GV1782.5.M36 2012
  792.82—dc22   2011001170

Cherry Lake Publishing would like to acknowledge
the work of The Partnership for 21st Century Skills.
Please visit *www.21stcenturyskills.org* for more information.

Printed in the United States of America
Corporate Graphics Inc.
July 2011
CLFA09

TABLE OF CONTENTS

CHAPTER ONE
MAKING ALL THE RIGHT MOVES

E merson and her friends took a break on the stage of their school auditorium. A local shoe store was

Choreographers help dancers tell a story.

filming a commercial there. Because the store sold dance shoes, the owners decided to put dancers in the commercial. Emerson and a few of her classmates took lessons through the school's tap dance program. They got to be the stars!

Emerson was excited to be in the commercial. She was also excited to work with a professional choreographer named Mr. Allen. He showed Emerson and the other dancers what to do in front of the cameras. He taught them a simple routine and showed them how to move on the stage. Mr. Allen also explained changes to the dance steps when the director decided to make the commercial shorter.

Emerson thought about what an amazing job Mr. Allen had. He used to be a professional dancer. Then he became a choreographer and created dances for other people to perform. His work helped Emerson shine during her first television commercial. It also made her think about becoming a choreographer herself!

Like Mr. Allen, some choreographers spend their time on commercial sets. Others oversee **auditions** and create dance moves for television shows, movies, and stage **productions**. Some choreographers teach at schools that train professional dancers.

Choreographers develop new dances or **reinterpret** traditional ones. Choreographer Acia Gray is the cofounder and artistic director of the Tapestry Dance **Company** in

Austin, Texas. The company specializes in jazz, tap, and modern dance. She is also the president of the International Tap Association. Gray believes that her job is a lot like writing.

LEARNING & INNOVATION SKILLS

When people think of choreographers, they often imagine men and women who work on theater sets or in dance **studios**. But not all choreographers direct dancers. Some work with martial artists and actors to create fight scenes in movies. Others work with models in fashion shows.

Choreographers also work on other things besides movement. Sometimes they work on costume design and lighting. They might also choose the music or sound effects for a production.

"The choreographer is the artist telling a story through the language of dance," Gray explains. "Dancers . . . are the living 'words' of the story. Some choreographers write their stories before they get to **rehearsal** and then teach the steps.

A choreographer might adjust a dancer's body to suit the dance movements.

I like to wait and create on the dancers themselves. Their unique personalities, styles, and even the music they're dancing to can have a [powerful] effect on how I write that day."

Are you ready to discover more about how choreographers spend their days?

This choreographer touches up a dancer's makeup before a performance.

Choreographers must consider the content and style of the story or message performers are expressing.

CHAPTER TWO
FROM AUDITION TO OPENING NIGHT

Ana checked her laptop to see who was auditioning next. The auditions would help her find backup

Choreographers attend rehearsals to help dancers perfect their movements.

dancers for a musical that she was choreographing. Afterward, she wanted to spend some time warming up.

Ana had to perform a series of new dance steps at rehearsal later in the afternoon. It was up to her to show these new steps to the dancers. Ana planned on speaking to the musical's director after rehearsal was over. He had asked her to **modernize** the steps that were traditionally used for a certain song. She had given a lot of thought to his request and was sure that she had the perfect idea.

Finally, Ana planned to wrap up her day by enjoying dinner with a fellow choreographer. The two of them hoped one day to start their own modern dance company. As Ana watched another dancer audition, she realized what a busy and fulfilling career she had.

Like Ana, some choreographers have jobs with theater groups. Others are involved with dance, film, television, and opera companies. A choreographer's exact responsibilities may change from day to day. For example, things tend to be busier just before a big performance. But many choreographers often have action-packed schedules even if they are months away from opening night.

They spend time discussing productions with everyone from directors and producers to composers, conductors, and lyricists. They might also deal with costume, set, and lighting designers. Choreographers need to be sure that a dance performance fits the production's overall theme. It is especially important that they keep this goal in mind as they create or revise dances.

During auditions, choreographers pay close attention to the dancers who are trying out. The dancers are hoping to join a company or win a part in a production. Choreographers compare their strengths and weaknesses. They know what dance styles and **techniques** will shape a performance. They can judge which dancers will best match their needs.

Auditions can be both exciting and stressful for choreographers and hopeful performers.

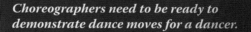

Choreographers need to be ready to demonstrate dance moves for a dancer.

After dancers are hired, choreographers teach them the routines they have created or revised. This is not always an easy task. Dance steps are usually not written down on paper the same way words or musical notes are. This means choreographers often show dancers what moves to make by demonstrating them during rehearsals.

"I rehearse with my company 35 hours or more per week," says Acia Gray. "I spend time warming the dancers up, teaching and refining technique." Gray also notes that her schedule becomes busier before big performances. She describes this period as being like the "editing stage of a book." It is when she must figure out production details and help performers adjust to last-minute choreography changes.

A choreographer demonstrates the emotion she wants a dancer to express.

Choreographers may not spend as much time in front of audiences as professional dancers do. Still, they have to take good care of their bodies. They often have to demonstrate new routines to dancers. Hectic schedules keep choreographers on their feet most of the day.

"All [dancers and choreographers] need to warm up their muscles and their minds," explains Acia Gray. "A healthy dancer or choreographer is strong. Rest, good food, and a healthy lifestyle make a big difference in the quality of a professional's work."

"A performance always involves adding new material and 'cleaning' the choreography," she explains. The choreographer and performers spend extra time in the theater. They need to make sure that the lights, music, and special effects are all timed just right.

Choreographers need **stamina** and organizational skills to keep up with their busy schedules. Daily rehearsals for a professional dance performance can last between three and eight hours. Sometimes companies have several performances a day. This means that choreographers have to be in good physical shape. They have to be able to dance and stay on their feet for long stretches of time. They also need the mental energy to react quickly when asked to change a routine.

Choreographers need to wear shoes and clothes that allow people to see exactly the movements that they are making. This may mean dressing in a leotard and slippers to perform a ballet routine. It could also mean putting on exercise pants, a tank top, and tap shoes to do a tap number. Each style of dance has certain clothing that works best.

Tools such as digital cameras, video recorders, and computers all come in handy for choreographers. They can be used to capture and play back details from auditions, rehearsals, and performances. This makes it easy for choreographers to study carefully their dancers' movement. It helps them determine which parts of the choreography need to be improved or replaced. Can you picture yourself reviewing the dance moves for a hit **Broadway** show or a popular music video? You're about to learn how some men and women make these dreams come true!

Choreographers often wear clothing that allows them to move freely.

CHAPTER THREE
BECOMING A CHOREOGRAPHER

Tim understood exactly how tired and nervous the dancers in his company were. It was the first time most of them would

A choreographer talks with his dancers during a rehearsal.

be performing on a professional stage. As their choreographer and artistic director, Tim had spent months working with them. First, he taught them the choreography for the ballet they were to perform. As artistic director, he helped them prepare for the performance. The ballet would take place in just a few days. Tickets were already sold out.

Tim could relate to the mixture of emotions he saw in the dancers' faces. He had once been in their shoes. He spent 10 years performing ballet professionally before becoming a choreographer. During that time, he took courses in choreography at a nearby dance academy. Tim also danced with several companies before forming his own.

These experiences and his knowledge of ballet helped Tim become an effective choreographer. He was patient with his dancers and his production crew. Tim was also self-disciplined. As artistic director, he made sure that everyone in the company stuck to an organized rehearsal schedule. This included a warm-up routine and extra time to discuss any changes to the choreography. Tim's background and abilities were leading him down a promising career path. Thanks to his skills, he was also helping others to be successful in their careers.

Like Tim, most choreographers begin as professional dancers. This allows them to learn about the styles and techniques used to create and reinterpret dances. Some dancers begin attending movement classes at a very young age. Teenagers might spend summers training at professional dance academies. Dancers often start full-time classes at these academies after graduating from high school.

LIFE & CAREER SKILLS

Not all choreographers need to study at a dance academy or earn a college degree to find work. But this type of education improves a choreographer's career opportunities and chances of doing well. Some choreographers take courses in history, literature, art, and music. These classes help them to understand better certain productions and performances. In addition, choreographers need academic degrees to get jobs as instructors at certain schools and academies.

Other dancers enroll in colleges that offer degrees in dance. Dance academies and college programs sometimes feature courses in choreography. Still, many choreographers gain their most valuable experience by auditioning and performing as dancers.

"There are many different avenues to becoming a professional who works in choreography," says Acia Gray. "The best advice I can give to someone who is interested in

Dance students sometimes gain experience by performing in university productions.

this career is to identify a choreographer or school that they admire and want to grow and create with. Then get involved with them on any level you can."

People hoping to build careers in choreography often try to get jobs as assistants to well-known choreographers. Some save enough money to start their own dance companies. Others work as **freelancers**. A small percentage of choreographers have full-time jobs. But the majority go from job to job. All choreographers must spend time **networking** with dance companies and film, television, and theater producers.

Being a choreographer requires patience, creativity, and problem-solving skills. People who work in choreography

Choreographers work alongside many people, including directors, conductors, and dancers.

must be able to think and react quickly. Organization is also very important. Choreographers must keep track of many different parts of a performance, from dance moves to stage lighting.

Finally, choreographers need to understand the value of teamwork. They work with a wide range of professionals, from performers and producers to sound and lighting technicians. Choreographers aren't likely to advance in their field if they don't respect and encourage the people around them.

What kind of money should a potential choreographer expect to make? In May 2008, the U.S. Bureau of Labor Statistics reported that choreographers' salaries ranged from less than $17,880 a year to more than $67,160 a year. The middle 50 percent had an annual income that was between $25,320 and $55,360.

Earnings depend on the choreographer's level of experience. They also depend on what organization the choreographer works for and whether the job is long-term or short-term. Some choreographers are members of **unions**. Unions guarantee that members will receive certain benefits and wages.

Choreography is more than just creating a few dance steps. It takes dedication, talent, and skill to create or reshape a dance and direct the people performing it. If you're still determined to become a choreographer, you might want to hear what experts predict about the future of this career!

CHAPTER FOUR
LOOKING TOWARD THE FUTURE

Lucy hoped to one day choreograph music videos. Her mom had a successful career as a choreographer

Teaching dance is one way to make extra money when starting out as a choreographer.

and loved her work. But she told Lucy that finding jobs in choreography had become very challenging. She predicted that things might get even tougher in the years ahead.

Lucy thought her mom was one of the most talented people she knew. But even she faced competition in her career. She freelanced as a choreographer. This meant she was always making phone calls and attending networking events to find new jobs. If work was slow, Lucy's mom sometimes taught hip-hop lessons at a local studio to earn extra money. But she stayed committed to living out her dream no matter what challenges she experienced. When Lucy watched her mom's music videos, she knew that she wanted to do the exact same thing.

Like Lucy and her mom, people who hope to build careers in choreography need to be dedicated and willing to network. Competition for jobs is fierce, and talent alone does not guarantee success. The U.S. Department of Labor estimates that job opportunities for professional dancers and choreographers will increase by only about 6 percent between 2008 and 2018. This rate of growth is slower than it is for many other careers.

The intense job competition means that choreographers often have trouble finding long-term work. Dance and production companies hire few choreographers on a permanent basis. Choreographers who don't get these permanent jobs have to spend a lot of time looking for work.

In addition, decreased funding for dance and production companies will probably continue to limit the number of new choreography jobs. Some choreographers also worry that the dance industry will be harmed by the growing use of computers and other technology.

"We seem to be slowly moving away from physical face-to-face communication," says Acia Gray. "I hope I'm

Music and computer graphics can help a choreographer visualize a dance.

wrong [and] that the human body [through dance] becomes more of an important communication tool and not less." On the other hand, technology has provided new opportunities to record and review auditions, rehearsals, and performances. New software also allows choreographers to create and teach dance moves with computer animation.

21ST CENTURY CONTENT

Can you think of any other ways that technology might impact choreographers? You may have already experienced this while watching television or Internet videos! The past few years have seen an increase in shows about dancing. *Dancing with the Stars* and *So You Think You Can Dance* are two popular examples. These shows are helping people learn more about dancers, choreographers, and their career paths.

Perhaps you'll soon find yourself trying to figure out a routine for a music video. Or maybe you'll be showing your dance class a new step you created. There are countless career paths for you to choose from if you want to become a choreographer! Which one will you take?

Twyla Tharp receives applause following a performance.

SOME FAMOUS CHOREOGRAPHERS

George Balanchine (1904–1983) was born in Russia but became especially well known for his choreography after moving to the United States in the 1930s. He cofounded the famous New York City Ballet in 1948. His work with the company revealed his knowledge of classical dance techniques. He was even more widely recognized for helping to modernize ballet.

Agnes De Mille (1905–1993) earned fame for her lasting impact on musical theater. She was born in New York City and choreographed productions such as *Oklahoma!* and *Brigadoon*. She often used dance to explore characters' emotions and identities. To her, choreography was about more than just showing off dancers' physical skills. Creating and revising dances was a chance to add to the story as it played out onstage.

Robert Louis "Bob" Fosse (1927–1987) worked as an actor, director, screenwriter, and dancer, and was also a famous and respected choreographer. He was born in Chicago, Illinois. Starting in the 1940s, he began a career in jazz performance that lasted nearly four decades. His talent won him praise on Broadway stages and Hollywood film sets. He won eight Tony Awards for choreography. He is perhaps best remembered for choreographing the musicals *Chicago* and *Cabaret*.

Twyla Tharp (1941–) was born in Portland, Indiana. She is viewed as one of America's leading female choreographers. She has built a successful career in both stage and film productions. She has worked on musicals, such as *Singin' in the Rain*, and on films, such as *Amadeus* and *Hair*. She is skilled at blending a wide variety of dance styles together within a single performance.

GLOSSARY

auditions (aw-DIH-shuhnz) performances that dancers give in the hopes of winning a part in a production

Broadway (BRAWD-way) a street in New York City that is the center of a world-famous theater district

company (KUHM-puh-nee) an organization of dancers or other performers

freelancers (FREE-lant-suhrz) workers who provide professional services to several employers without having a long-term contract with any of them

modernize (MAH-dur-nyze) to bring something up-to-date

networking (NET-wur-king) communicating within a group in the hopes of creating beneficial professional relationships

productions (pruh-DUHK-shuhnz) plays, dance performances, or other shows that are presented to an audience

rehearsal (ri-HUR-suhl) a practice session that occurs before a performance

reinterpret (re-uhn-TUHR-pruht) tell a story or express a message from a new perspective

stamina (STAH-muh-nuh) lasting strength and energy

studios (STU-dee-ohz) spaces for teaching and practicing dance

techniques (tek-NEEKS) ways of doing something to create different styles of dance

unions (YOON-yuhnz) organizations of employees that bargain with employers for benefits and pay requirements

FOR MORE INFORMATION

BOOKS

Joosten, Michael. *Dance and Choreography*. New York: Rosen Central, 2010.

Murphy, Liz. *A Dictionary of Dance*. Maplewood, NJ: Blue Apple Books, 2007.

Reeves, Diane Lindsey, and Lindsey Clasen. *Career Ideas for Kids Who Like Music and Dance*. New York: Checkmark Books, 2007.

WEB SITES

Acia Gray
www.aciagray.com
Visit this Web page for a closer look at choreographer Acia Gray's life and career.

United States Department of Labor: Bureau of Labor Statistics—Dancers and Choreographers
www.bls.gov/oco/ocos094.htm
Check out this site for fast facts and stats about careers in dance and choreography.

INDEX

ABOUT THE AUTHOR

Katie Marsico has written more than 80 books for young readers. She dedicates this book to her dear friends, colleagues, and mentors, Pam and Russ.